TALKING AS FAST AS I CAN

THE HIGHLY SENSITIVE PERSON CONVERSATION SKILLS MANUAL FOR QUIET INTROVERTS

I0456199

BY SMART READS

Free Audiobook

As a thank you for being a Smart Reader you can choose 2 FREE audiobooks from audible.com. Simply sign up for free by visiting www.audibletrial.com/Travis to get your books.

Visit:
www.smartreads.co/freebooks
to receive Smart Reads books for FREE

Check us out on Instagram:
www.instagram.com/smart_readers
@smart_readers

ABOUT SMARTREADS

Choose Smart Reads and get smart every time. Smart Reads sorts through all the best content and condenses the most helpful information into easily digestible chunks.

We design our books to be short, easy to read and highly informative. Leaving you with maximum understanding in the least amount of time.

Smart Reads aims to accelerate the spread of quality information so we've taken the copyright off everything we publish and donate our material directly to the public domain. You can read our uncopyright below.

We believe in paying it forward and donate 5% of our net sales to Pencils of Promise to build schools, train teachers and support child education.

To limit our footprint and restore forests around the globe we are planting a tree for every 10 hardcover books we sell.

Thanks for choosing Smart Reads and helping us help the planet.

Sincerely,

Travis & the Smart Reads Team

TABLE OF CONTENTS

INTRODUCTION

There's always that person who can come to a party without knowing anyone and instantly begin chatting and laughing with complete strangers, as if they had known these people all their lives. Meanwhile, you might be in a corner of the room struggling to say something fun and interesting to someone you've known for a while.

You feel awkward, miserable, wishing you were somewhere or somebody else. For some people, it can be hard to make friends and strike up relationships. These people often thing they're not interesting and resign themselves to just get used to not having many friends.

Well, that's couldn't be more wrong. The fact is, EVERYONE is interesting, including you. Even if you may not be the "bell of the ball" right away, there are ways to bring out your wonderful personality.

In this book, you will find techniques to increase your confidence, dust off the ol' charm, and communicate comfortably, both with people you know and people you have never met before.

You will learn how to make others feel at ease around you, projecting a positive, confident image, reading the body language of other people and maintaining positive relationships.

None of this will be based on hype, false confidence or invention. This book will help you discover the wonderful you and bring out your own personality and enjoy the company of others.

CHAPTER 1: BEING SHY

You're invited to a party. You don't really want to go. The thought of meeting lots of people you've never met before makes you nervous. You dread interacting in a group because you always feel awkward.

You'd rather stay home and watch TV with the dog, but you do really wish you could go out and have a great time, like others seem to do. You envy people who seem to chat and make small talk with ease. They're laughing, making jokes.

Rest assured, you're not alone. Now you may ask yourself, "What's wrong with me? Why can't I fit in? I'm a misfit! A social failure!"

Hold it right there. Let's dissect a few myths about this situation before we go on.
What you're experiencing is not that uncommon. A lot people experience shyness and awkwardness in social situations, even those who are professional socialites. The list of actors, singers, politicians, businesspeople, and others in the public eye who feel the same might astonish you. This list includes Brad Pitt, Carol Burnett, Johnny Depp, Elton John, Steven Spielberg, Michelle Pfeiffer, Cher and Tom Hanks.

Actor and comedian Jim Carrey once said, "I know this sounds strange, but as a kid, I was really shy. Painfully shy. The turning point was freshman year, when I was the biggest geek alive. No one, I mean no one, even talked to me."

Stephen Spielberg also felt the same way. He says, "I never felt comfortable with myself, because I was never part of the majority. I always felt awkward and shy and on the outside of the momentum of my friends' lives."

Many people in the public eye talk about their occupations being a mask for their shyness. A stand-up comedian may appear full of confidence, but he's performing. He's doing a job that prevents him from truly revealing himself. He's in his comfort zone and doesn't have to interact with others.

Jarvis Cocker said that he formed a band because of "feelings of shyness and social ineptitude." He adds, "I saw it as some way of being able to interact with people from a safe distance."

When you are in company you may not have such a persona to hide behind but you probably know people who use such a shield. You're likely familiar with people who constantly makes jokes without saying anything about themselves. You've likely also met individuals who come up with extraordinary stories that couldn't possibly be true. This is another method of protection. Remember, social awkwardness is not a sign of abnormality.

Another myth to dispel is that shyness is unattractive. Shy people tend to be sensitive to others. They are also adaptable, and contrary to appearances and expectations, adjust well to changing social conditions.

Socially anxious people tend to plan for the future and avoid unnecessary risks. They also tend to be sociable and are good at calming things down. What's more, they are also stable. Shy people tend to be empathetic, because they understand pain and being misunderstood. People also tend to trust shy people, because they aren't perceived to be motivated by self-aggrandizement.

In terms of work, shy persons enjoy solitary work, and as this requires special responsibility, they tend to be reliable too. A lot of truck drivers, astronomers, bus drivers, and writers are socially timid.

Both introverts and extroverts can experience shyness. By introvert, this means someone who draws strength and inspiration from their own mental resources (not people who are obsessed with themselves). By extrovert, this is someone who thrives on external stimuli and relationships with other people.

Shyness may be an even worse torture for an extrovert than for an introvert. Extroverts need the stimulation they derive from social interaction yet feel incapable of satisfying that need.

All that aside however, there is a downside to shyness and social anxiety. You know this. Otherwise you wouldn't be reading this book. People who are extremely shy be lonely. Apart from not being very fun, loneliness can lead to mental health problems. It can prevent an individual from achieving their desires, goals and dreams. This also makes going out on that first date almost impossible. They end up missing out on opportunities to have fun. And also miss out on the advantages that social connections may offer, like advancing their career, furthering business interests, gaining credibility and influence in social circles.

Now, this book doesn't claim to miraculously cure you of your shyness. Shyness can stem from a lot of things. At other times it can be a serious disorder such as a Social Anxiety Disorder, which is an intense anxiety in social situations that can manifest itself physically. If you think you may be suffering from this please do read this book but also visit your doctor.

It's important to remember that nothing in this book will try and change your personality or make you someone you're not. It's all about bringing out you and letting you shine in all your beauty, magnificence and charm.

CHAPTER 2: CAUSES OF SHYNESS

Why are people shy? This is an important question to ask yourself because if you can address the root cause of your shyness your social interactions will improve. Of course, there are countless possible reasons for shyness.

Many people sometimes have a lack of self-confidence resulting in them being shy. Sometimes they may have a negative image of themselves and believe other people can see their perceived inferiorities. But apart from the sheer mathematical improbability of being inferior to every person on the planet, the inferiority lives entirely on the person's own imagination. Of course, it may be reinforced by negative experiences and relationships. A family member may have told you constantly that you were a dumb child. And at some point, you ended up believing it.

At times, people wish to be perfect in everything they say and do. They are dismayed by what they perceive as failures in their interactions. Perhaps they offended someone, or said the wrong word. And so, they discourage themselves from engaging with people in the first place.

Don't try to be perfect because it's impossible. Everyone fails. Failure is natural and human – very human. It's also human not to admit to failure, so you might think you're the only person who makes mistakes. Everyone finds life a bit tricky!
Often people may not have the social skills and this may be due to upbringing and education. Deafness and other physical disabilities can also make you nervous in social situations. It is perfectly OK to say, "I'm hard of hearing. Would you mind speaking a little louder?"

It is true that a great many people are nervous when interacting with people with disabilities. This can be hard for people living with a disability who often suffer social isolation because of prejudices. That issue is easily the subject of another book. Suffice it to say, ignorance can be remedied, and generally if people see you are comfortable in yourself they will be comfortable with you too. You may want to explain to someone looking a little nervous, "Yeah, I understand this is a little confronting, but its okay. Talk to me like you would talk to anyone else."

Whatever the cause of your shyness, it is important to understand and address the underlying issue as well as force yourself to interact with people.

CHAPTER 3: FIRST IMPRESSIONS

First impressions are important. It's a bit of a cliché, but it's true. It is also true that you can't judge people by appearances. People who are initially unimpressive can turn out be the most wonderful friends.

Alas, however, most people will form judgments at the first meeting. That is why John Smith turns up to an interview in a shirt and tie with neatly combed hair, even though he's happiest in jeans and a tee, an old pair of sneakers and scraggly hair. However this isn't about inventing a persona for others to see. No, you want people to see the real you, au naturel.

Even when John Smith presents himself to a prospective employer looking like he was dressed for a wedding, he wants the employer to see him. His clothes speak about the person he wants to be in the company. So it is with you when meeting somebody for the first time. You don't want to be somebody you're not. You want that person to see you, and you want your image to enhance who you are.

You can start thinking about the person you want people to see, that is, the real you. Many of people spend years trying to work out who they are. In fact, so many people aren't comfortable with their own image. If you aren't confident about yourself, you can't project confidence. So think about who you are and how you want others to see you.

Suppose you're a little flamboyant. You enjoy a colorful turn of phrase and you like dressing up. If that's the case, why do you wear plain clothes? Perhaps you would like to add a splash of color. Wear a colorful scarf, or a red jacket, or a stylish fedora. They may make you stand out in a crowd and give you confidence in your personality.

On the other hand, perhaps you spend a lot of time grooming and choosing stylish clothes that you're never comfortable in, because you want to appear trendy. But maybe you'd be more comfortable going to that party in a plaid shirt over a tee, with jeans and your favorite Nikes.

There's also social convention to consider. Someone turning up to a wedding in jeans and a crop-top is not likely to create a good impression. Similarly a person presenting himself or herself at a picnic in a jacket, tie and shiny black shoes will be talked about, but possibly for the wrong reasons!
There are of course some things about a human being that are perfectly natural but which should not intrude themselves into polite society. People's state of

hygiene should never give offence and grooming should give the appearance that you care about yourself, your appearance, and others. The style of your grooming should of course reflect what you're comfortable with and the occasion. All this is just good manners and etiquette, which is what a great deal of this book is about.

So you've taken care of clothing and grooming. Next consider your body language.
Body language is terribly significant in your relationships, though most people underestimate its significance.

When you meet somebody for the first time, your body language gives away volumes. For example, if someone doesn't give eye contact they are giving the impression that they don't want to engage in a conversation, even though the truth may be, as it often is, that the person they've met is a bit shy and nervous. Many people unfortunately don't recognize shyness.

Think about your arms too. When you cross your arms you often give the impression that you're being defensive and that you don't want to engage. Folding arms is a natural defensive response. You protect your most vulnerable body part, the chest. Lowering your arms shows people you don't fear them and that you are open to them.

If you don't know what to do with your hands, you can put them in your pants pockets, if you are comfortable with that, or hold them behind your back or hold the shoulder strap of a purse or bag you might be carrying. Remember too that a smile is a powerful thing. People immediately look at the face. They read the eyes and the mouth to see if someone wants to engage in conversation. A smile will invite them, and they usually respond with a smile too, which will help break down any inhibitions you might have.

Be mindful of your handshake too. This is a very important opportunity to make a good impression, because when meeting somebody for the first time many people will offer you their hand.

People will often judge a person by their handshake and some rude people will comment on a weak handshake. Others will crush the life out of a hand. Sometimes they don't know they are doing it. Often they are being aggressive, especially if they purposely grip the hand.

Your handshake need only be firm. A firm handshake says "Hello. Here I am. Let's talk." It need not say anything less or more.

Nowadays a lot of people, especially the young, will often hug strangers or kiss women they don't know on the cheek. If you're uncomfortable with this, that's fine. A good part of etiquette consists in respecting personal space. If you see someone about to embrace you and you don't want them to do it, warmly offer your hand instead.

On the subject of personal space, this is important to consider too. The zone of personal comfort will vary from person to person and there is no hard and fast rule. Generally speaking, individuals are comfortable in a social setting with the other person being 1to 2 meters away. If you are too close you may make the other person uncomfortable. If you are too far away you may give the impression that you are uncomfortable.

You will find that you can read the other's body's language and gauge their level of comfort. You can then subtly adjust the distance between you.

CHAPTER 4: KEEPING THAT GOOD IMPRESSION

So you're at a party. Someone you've never met before has noticed you and approached you. You've made eye contact. Your body posture isn't defensive and you've got a great smile. All in all you've made a great first impression.

As mentioned, non-verbal communication is every bit as powerful as verbal conversation and in fact, more so.

Suppose you're speaking with a tradesman and he's telling you that he will repair your roof within three weeks and at half the price of his competitors. While he's saying this he is looking away from me and scratching his nose. This is a big clue that he may be lying to you. Now it may be that he is an avid birdwatcher and has just seen a rare Yellow-bellied Tit sitting on a tree nearby. He may be scratching because he is allergic to the cashmere sweater you are wearing.

Be that as it may, your first impression will be that he is trying to pull a fast one. So body language is important.

Here are a few tips. Don't fidget. That gives the impression you're bored and would rather be somewhere else. You're probably nervous and that's understandable. Try putting your hands in your pockets, as suggested earlier, or hold them behind your back, or use hand gestures if they are natural for you.

The question of what degree of physical contact to use in a conversation is a tricky one. Some gregarious people will be forever touch you and this can be very annoying. It is also possible to give an altogether wrong impression about the nature of the relationship you wish to establish. On the other hand, someone can be perfectly warm and engaging without making any body contact beyond the standard handshake. So it will depend on what is natural and comfortable for you and the other person.

It's best to have no physical contact at all until you've established a level of intimacy in which you both feel comfortable, and this will happen quite naturally.

Another thing to remember is that when someone is talking, it is important to listen. Many people hear another person speaking but they are not listening. You likely know people who ignore what you are saying and would rather talk about themselves and the things that interest them. It is not that they find you boring. If they did they would find an excuse to leave you. Rather they are more interested in themselves and haven't given you a chance. They are the ones being boring.

You can easily identify good listeners. They nod or otherwise express agreement at various points in the conversation, maintain eye contact, mirror the speaker's feelings (e.g. "Really? How awful!" or "That's awesome!"), and don't try to divert the conversation.

If you show interest in what the other person has to say they are more likely to be interested in what you have to say.

CHAPTER 5: STARTING A CONVERSATION

The hardest thing about a conversation can be starting it. Most people are often nervous and they want to give a good impression. It's no surprise they want to be liked and don't want to appear awkward.

These fears are natural. Many people will not speak to strangers if they can avoid it because they are more comfortable with people they know. Chances are the person you want to speak with is feeling the same thing. Psychologists say that 40% of people experience shyness in social situations.

There are people who are extremely nervous and shy when speaking to strangers or if they are approached by a stranger. And their reaction sometimes comes across as silly. Many people who don't understand think it's an unusual reaction. But for the person experiencing it, the shyness is real and they have to deal with it all the time until they overcome it.

So how to break the ice in a new social encounter? Well, you needn't rack your brains trying to think of something clever or witty or impressive to say. For a start you set yourself up having to continue to be clever and witty throughout the conversation, and that might be hard work.

Secondly, you don't want to appear as if you're trying to impress people because that doesn't impress anyone at all. It may also make conversation for the other person difficult. If you were to say, for example, "What do you think of the present situation in the Middle East? I think the Secretary of State hit the nail on the head, don't you?" The person you are speaking with might not have the slightest idea what's going on in the Middle East and just not interested.

Instead open with something simple like introducing yourself instead. The other person will usually reply by introducing himself or herself as well. You might then comment on the occasion and say, "It's a good party, isn't it?" or "They make a lovely couple don't they?" depending on the occasion and circumstances.

Once you've followed these social conventions you can find some common ground to talk about. A good question to ask is, "What do you do?" Now even if you're not a brain surgeon or into waste management like your new acquaintance is, chances are, you'll also have the opportunity to talk about your own occupation. If the other speaker is polite they will usually ask about it anyway.

As you talk, you will find more common ground. The other person might mention his or her interest in gardening and you might be interested in gardening too. You might share interests in fashion, sports, renovation, fishing or any number of subjects.

Taking the plunge is the hardest part. When you jump into the pool, it's always freezing for the first few moments. Afterwards you start to enjoy the water. When you are psyching yourself to take the plunge, ask yourself "What is the worst thing that could possibly happen?" Okay, you may get tongue-tied. Sure, the guy or girl might not be interested in talking. But you tried. And for every time you don't succeed there will be a time when you do.

If you're serious about overcoming your shyness, it's best to be deliberate about it. One method you can use to overcome your fear of conversation is to speak to at least one stranger every day. And by speaking, it means initiating the conversation. Buying a loaf of bread and newspaper from the local store doesn't count, because that is a conventional interaction. The idea is to reach beyond your comfort zone.

You can say something to someone while waiting at a bus stop, like, "The buses are never on time, are they?" Or you can smile and say hello to a stranger you pass by on the street, even compliment someone on their hat while waiting in a queue.

The advantage of this is that the people you encounter are strangers whom you'll probably never see again. You can experiment with them. Sometimes you may be a little red-faced after an interaction that didn't work well but as long as they're not calling the police then what does it matter?

After a while of doing this, you'll notice that none of these strangers could hurt you or injure your feelings. In fact, none of them want to. You'll also notice that most will respond in a positive manner and that will help boost your confidence.

Remember that you only truly fail when you fail to try. Finding the courage to try and be what you can be is success in itself. So get out there and give it a go. You'll surprise yourself!

CHAPTER 6: KEEPING 'EM KEEN

Chances are, you will meet people you want to talk to for a while and perhaps you won't see them again. Then there are people you want to talk again and again. The latter may be persons you find attractive or those you find interesting. Perhaps you want to establish a relationship for business or career reasons. Sometimes, you just find conversation with them stimulating and interesting.

In this chapter, you will learn strategies that will encourage these people to want to talk to you again. You want them to remember your conversation and your face. Remember that people generally love to hear about themselves in conversation. They also enjoy being valued. Hence, it's important to hone your listening skills. Hear what they have to say. Latch onto something that is of importance or interest to the other speaker (and ideally to you as well) and make that the subject of conversation.

If for example someone mentions they have a sore leg because they strained it while landscaping their garden, then you can ask about landscaping. What are you doing? What's your plan? How long have you being doing it? If you're into landscaping too, all the better.

Try to use open-ended questions. Open-ended questions are those that can't be answered with just a yes or no. For example, if you say, "Are you enjoying the party?" The answer might be "No" and the conversation stops, unless you're willing to ask them why they aren't enjoying the party and they tell you their Aunt Mildred just died. This is a closed question.

However, if you were to ask, "These party decorations are so colorful. What do you think of them?" You are inviting the speaker into a conversation, because they can't answer yes or no. They might say, "They're giving me a headache" or "They're simply gorgeous." This is an example of an open-ended question.

It can be also useful to remember things you've learnt about somebody in a conversation and bring them up again in future conversations. For example, someone you're speaking with may mention his or her love of fishing. Afterwards you can do some research on fishing. In the next conversation you might mention the 55-pound pike caught by a West German in 1986 (true fact). A warning though if you're going to research – make sure you know your subject well. Otherwise you may find yourself in trouble.

CHAPTER 7: LETTING YOURSELF SHINE

The idea that you are somehow unlikeable and uninteresting lurks isn't something unique to your mind, a good many people also think of the same thing about themselves. Even the most witty and fascinating people often consider themselves complete bores and unworthy of attention.

In fact, anxiety about your self-image is common, about 50% of the human race harbor negative thoughts about themselves in company. Many, perhaps, don't like who they are and are afraid that people will somehow see through the "charade." This means of course that if you are anxious about a conversation there is a 50% chance that your conversational partner is too.

But ask yourself how many people you've strangled in the subway. How many children have you stolen ice cream from? When was the last time you killed a chicken and offered it to Beelzebub? None? Never?

If you think about it, you've got decent, even endearing qualities. You've done interesting things. You know interesting stuff. In fact, you may have qualities, relationships, occupations and knowledge that would elicit envy in any number of people!

So in your conversations don't hide who you are and what your beliefs and opinions are. People are attracted to people who know who they are and state their opinions. On the other hand, people generally don't respect those who constantly agree with them or who don't assert their own opinions. Mind you, you must respect other people, and though you may disagree with someone else's views you can agreeably discuss them.

The best conversations are those where you end up learning someone else's point of view, think about it for yourself and see if it's something you can agree with or not. You'll learn a lot of things and your worldview might change or at least grow.

Sometimes people spruce up conversation with exaggeration and – let's face it -outright lies.

"I was Employee of the Month five times last year." (Well, it was two, actually.)

"Oh, I think she's such a wonderful person!" (Thinks – when she isn't sniping.)

Many of us do it, but there's no need to. Let the truth be truth. It shows your confidence. It shows you are comfortable with yourself. And that's powerful. That's classy. Truth has a fascinating attraction. Of course, this doesn't mean you have to go around telling everything to everyone. You will need to be discreet and people don't need to know everything about your life.

There are times when it can be challenging to skirt around issues you don't want to talk about or be a part of. For instance, people would start criticizing other people you know. This can be awkward. You don't want to offend the talker by cutting them off and you don't want to harm the person he's talking about by participating in malicious talk. During these times, it's important to learn how to politely change the subject. If someone else is around, you can greet him or her and invite them to join you. Then the talker has to stop sniping and change the subject. You can of course also just politely tell the talker, "I'm sorry, but I would rather not get into this topic."

When you're feeling anxious in a conversation you can explain this to the person you're talking to. Anxiety in conversation is a real thing, experienced by more people than you might imagine. Indeed, in some people it can produce real fear. Unfortunately few people recognize social discomfort for what it is. If you are fidgeting, averting your eyes or shuffling your feet and even not saying much, people often think you don't want to talk.

You could explain that you are feeling nervous and you're not trying to avoid them. This does have its risks. You don't know how the other person is going to react. They could feel uncomfortable themselves and find an excuse to leave, or hopefully they find your candor refreshing and know exactly what to do. There are people who are very good at putting other people at ease. You will have to take it by situation. But remember, however a person reacts, if you choose to say you're anxious, they are responsible for their reaction. You aren't.

Don't worry about how your conversation partner is going to react to the things you say or do. This is good advice for life in general. You are responsible for your actions and feelings. Everyone else is responsible for his or her own actions and feelings. So be true to yourself and don't worry about what others think. What does it matter if she doesn't like your dress? You love it! That's what counts. Be yourself. Honesty and openness is attractive. Deception and disguise isn't. In any case, if you pretend to be someone you're not, you will be found out eventually.

CHAPTER 8: INTIMACY

So you've begun a first conversation. It went well. Your conversation partner is interested in you. Why not? You're an interesting person. How do you advance to a deeper level of intimacy in conversation?

This is something you really can't force. You both have to be ready, and if it is meant to be it will happen naturally. This isn't about romantic intimacy of course, but also about firm friendships. You can however introduce elements to your conversation that invite intimacy. If you both have a common interest this is a great starter. You can find out a lot about your partner by talking about things you both enjoy and are enthusiastic about. You may be in the same occupation. You might have gone on a holiday in the same place. Perhaps your kids go to the same school. You may both love Doctor Who and wax lyrical about Tom Baker's performance as the Fourth Doctor from 1974 – 1981. It's about this time when you can openly share your feelings and opinions.

Do be careful though about asking personal questions about the other person, their family and history and the like, unless of course they volunteer the information. You do not want to make your conversation partner uncomfortable. It is also wise to avoid controversial topics like religion and politics, unless, again, the person volunteers his or her opinion.

You will want to show the other person that you are concerned for their welfare, so if you find you have crossed a boundary, simply apologize and change the subject. Most people will appreciate an apology, and if your conversation partner is interested in you, he or she will generally pass over the faux pas. Trust plays an important part in this level of conversation. If someone shares something personal about themselves to you, they are paying you a compliment. They believe, or at least, hope, that you can be trusted.

It goes almost without saying that you must respect that trust. It does happen however that you may mention in passing personal things you have learnt to other people. You may do this entirely without malice. You may be commiserating with someone, "Oh too bad. You got fired. You know, Julia got fired too. Just last week. The boss accused her of stealing from the till. "Did Julia give you permission to reveal that information? Well, she didn't say not to! Even so, you may presume you don't have permission. Broken confidences can cause damage to reputations as well as destroy trust.

On the other hand, revealing something personal about yourself can be powerful. You are telling the other person you trust them. You have exposed yourself and become vulnerable, and you are saying you have no fear of being betrayed.

The risk of course is that you actually may be betrayed. So you should start with a revelation that is fairly innocuous. It is best not to mention your morbid fear of Smurfs. Instead say something about yourself that is personal but not likely to cause you harm.

CHAPTER 9: RESCUING A CONVERSATION

Often conversations can drag. They are punctuated by awkward silences. Then one or both you suddenly remember that they have left the gas on at home or they've been diagnosed with a contagious tropical disease and they should go away.
How to manage those awkward moments?

Bear in mind you may really want to leave the conversation, and these silences can present an opportunity to end it. Bringing a conversation to an end may seem an art in itself, but there is really no need to make up an excuse. Neither is there any need to be brutally honest, such as "Well this conversation is flowing like cement, isn't?" A simple, "Well it was good to meet you" or "I'll move on now," is perfectly acceptable and will possibly relieve your partner who will offer no objection.

But how do you revive a conversation you want to prolong? One strategy is to use open-ended questions. You've read about this earlier. Also, once your partner answers a question you may want to probe the answer a little bit. Suppose you've asked about their vacation in India. They might answer, "It was awesome. Absolutely loved it." You can follow up with, "What was it about India that you liked so much? How long have you wanted to go? Tell me about your favorite experience." You've opened up a great vista of topics you can talk about.

Don't be afraid to talk about yourself and your experiences as well. Most people think it's somehow bad manners to draw attention to oneself. Habitually drawing the topic of conversation to oneself is boorish, but people often underestimate the interest our lives and experiences may generate. So once you've talked about the other person's experiences, talk about your experiences as well.

Another method of prolonging conversation is to parrot your partner. Punctuate his or her conversations with sounds and words that show you're listening and interested. You might say, "yes" or "uh-huh," or repeat what you perceive to be a key point, or simply nod. This tells the other person that you are interested in what he or she is saying.

What if you don't understand what they're saying? Don't nod off and act like you were listening or had any idea about what they were talking about when you don't. You will be caught at some point.
To avoid this faux pas it is perfectly acceptable to ask for clarification. "I'm sorry. I don't understand," or "Could you explain that please." This tells the speaker

that you are interested in what he or she is saying. You can also just say, "I'm sorry. My mind was somewhere else. Could you repeat that please?"

If you're in a group, ask the opinion of other members of the group. This injects fresh perspective into the conversation, and has the advantage of taking the pressure of you to keep the conversation going.

Many people find talking in a group daunting, but in fact it can be easier than talking one to one. You're not the continuous object of attention and indeed when starting out you may want to begin in a group and then build up your confidence to initiate a one-to-one conversation.

CHAPTER 10: ENDING A CONVERSATION

Sometimes people get into conversations they would rather avoid. You've likely met people who have taken you aside and started talking non-stop, and not about anything interesting. It's usually about themselves or their own interests or opinions.

Then there are the conversationalists who are continually complaining about some thing or another and maligning your friends and co-workers, and maybe even you. There are people who can criticize others (including you) in very subtle ways, such as, "Yes, I suppose that is a nice dress, though it would be so last year for me." Others are manipulative. They want something from you. They try to draw you into their particular office clique or try and convince you that Brian in accounting is fiddling the books or that the boss is seeing too much of Wanda in Sales.

There is no reason for you to suffer these conversations, especially if their end is to manipulate or malign. You want your conversations to be positive, reinforcing and uplifting.

Then of course you may really just need to end the conversation. You have an appointment and need to be somewhere else or have someone else to speak to.

You may have to pick up the kids from school or take grandma to emergency. Ending a conversation can be difficult, but a good rule to follow is to be direct and assertive. You don't need to be brutally honest or rude.

Wait for lulls in the conversation, those moments when there is a brief silence or someone has brought a point to a close and you have acknowledged and commented on it. Bring that part of the conversation to some kind of conclusion. But what do you actually say to end the conversation? Something like, "It's been lovely talking to you but I really must move on," is okay. The other person doesn't need to know why you're leaving. However, he or she may ask the reason you're going, and in this case you might want a few lines you can use, such as:

"I need to use the bathroom."
"I want to catch the speaker before he leaves."
"I must find my wife/ husband/ partner."
"I need to get to the grocery store before it closes."

Sometimes these excuses may not be strictly true and sometimes the other person will suspect they're not true. However they are part of social convention and are acceptable. And remember, people don't have the right to monopolize your time.

Some individuals will end conversations with statements that appear to defer to their conversational partner as if their conversations were somehow taking advantage of them.

For example, they might say, "I've already taken up too much of your time" or "I mustn't keep you away from your work" or "I'm sure you'll want to getting home now."

If you genuinely are anxious that you're taking too much of your acquaintance's time, then it's fine. But if it's an excuse, what you're really saying is that your partner is responsible for the end of the conversation, not you. Hence, it's best to defer from using those lines unless you mean it.

There are other things you can do to end conversations. You can introduce your partner to someone else, or have him introduce you to a third person. When someone joins the conversation stop speaking and allow them to speak. You may even prompt them. But whatever way you choose to end a conversation, always end with an appreciative tone.

"Thanks, Simon. This has been a very enlightening conversation."
"It was great catching up with you Sarah."

"It's been fun. We must do this again."

If you can, use the person's name. Shake hands. And if you want to meet the person again, then briefly make arrangements to do so. You may wish to exchange phone numbers. During this ritual be careful that the conversation doesn't resume, as it often does. If it does you may politely and warmly remind your partner of the reason you have to leave. You may also wish to step back a little from the person to indicate that you need to leave quickly.

CHAPTER 11: SOME HANDY HINTS

These are just a few hints to help with a conversation. No doubt you will find others, or come up with some of your own.

Keep a mental library of interesting or quirky facts in your head. You can insert these in a conversation when appropriate. For example, did you know the only cartoon character in The Simpsons to have five fingers on each hand is God? Every other hand only has four. Another fun fact is that goldfishes get seasick?

You could also memorize jokes. It also helps to memorize names. If you use someone's name in a conversation you will get his or her attention. People generally love hearing their own name in someone else's mouth.

Moreover, tell stories. Everyone loves stories. Instead of telling someone where you went on holiday, tell them a story about your holiday. Tell them how a monkey stole your passport in Morocco, or how you came across a magnificent elephant in Kenya.

You can have a few favorite stories ready to use. If you already know something about the person you're going to speak to you may wish to do a bit of preparation. What does the person do? Where do they live? What are their likes and dislikes, etc.

If you want to learn how to better speak confidently, consider joining a speechmaking club like Toastmasters International. Such a club will encourage you to speak confidently and argue coherently and persuasively.

However, whatever aids and tools you use do remember that the goal is to be able to participate in a fluid conversation naturally. So when you reach that level of ease (which you will!) those aids will no longer be necessary.

CONCLUSION

Hopefully this little book has given you some tips and encouragement on how to improve your conversations and your life.

As your conversations improve, your confidence will grow. Your success will increase your confidence. You will make a few mistakes too and that's fine. You can use these to improve. Even failures can be turned into triumphs.

Not only will your triumphs increase your confidence but your social standing too. You will become a master of yourself. You will be able to influence people and situations.

The most influential people have always been speakers and writers. Think of some of the great speeches and the women and men who made them. Consider Abraham Lincoln, Martin Luther King, Michelle Obama or Condoleezza Rice.

The powerful, confident you, will not be some creation. No, it will be the real you that has been hidden for so long. You will be able to ask for things without appearing weak or needing to go on bended knee. At the same time you won't be pushy or arrogant either. You will be able to build fulfilling, rewarding and advantageous relationships.

Good communication attracts interest. You will become more interesting and more popular. You will become more relaxed and hence gain more control of your life. With conversation skills you will gain windows into other people's worlds, experiences and possibilities.

This all sounds wonderful and you want to get there. However, give yourself time. It will be a long journey and it may be hard. But stay focused on what you want; don't be dismayed by little failures and disappointments.

Eventually, the rewards will come.

THANKS FOR READING

We really hope you enjoyed this book. If you found this material helpful feel free to share it with friends. You can also help others find it by leaving a review where you purchased the book. Your feedback will help us continue to write books you love.

The Smart Reads library is growing by the day! Make sure and check out the other wonderful books in our catalog. We would love to hear which books are your favorite.

Visit:
www.smartreads.co/freebooks
to receive Smart Reads books for FREE

Check us out on Instagram:
www.instagram.com/smart_readers
@smart_readers

Don't forget your 2 FREE audiobooks.
Use this link www.audibletrial.com/Travis to claim
your 2 FREE Books.

SMART READS ORIGINS

Smart Reads was born out of the desire to find the best information fast without having to wade through the sheer volume of fluff available online. Smart Reads combs through massive amounts of knowledge compiles the best into quick to read books on a variety of subjects.

We consider ourselves Smart Readers, not dummies. We know reading is smart. We're self taught. We like to learn a TON about a WIDE variety of topics. We have developed a love for books and we find intelligence attractive.

We found that each new topic we tried to learn about started with the challenge of finding the pieces of the puzzle that mattered most. It becomes a treasure hunt rather than an education.

Smart Reads wants to find the best of the best information for you. To condense it into a package that you can consume in an hour or less. So you can read more books about more topics in less time.

OUR MISSION

Smart Reads aims to accelerate the availability of useful information and will publish a high quality book on every major topic on amazon.

Smart Reads hopes to remove barriers to sharing by taking the copyright off everything we publish and donating it to the public domain. We hope other publishers and authors will follow our example.

Our goal is to donate $1,000,000 or more by 2020 to build over 2,000 schools by giving 5% of our net profit to Pencils of Promise.

We want to restore forests around the globe by planting a tree for every 10 physical books we sell and hope to plant over 100,000 trees by 2020.

Doesn't it feel good knowing that by educating yourself you are helping the world be a better place? We think so too...

Thanks for helping us help the world. You Smart Reader you...

Travis and the Smart Reads Team

WHY I STARTED SMART READS

Every time I wanted to learn about something new I'd have to buy 20 books on the topic and spend way too long sorting through them and reading them all until I arrived at the big picture. Until I had enough perspectives to know who was just guessing, who was uninformed and who had stumbled upon something remarkable.

I wished someone else could just go in and figure that out for me and tell me what matters. That's how smart reads was born. I want smart reads to be a company that does all that research up front. Sorts through all the content that is available on each topic and pulls out the most up to date complete understanding, then have people smarter than me package the best wisdom in an easy to understand way in the least amount of words possible.

For example, I got a new puppy so I wanted to learn about dog training. I bought 14 different books about dog training and by the time I got through the first 5 and finally started getting the big picture on the best way to train my puppy she had grown up into a dog.

Yeah she's well behaved. She doesn't poop in the house. I can get her to sit and come when I call. But what if someone else went in and read all those books for me, found the underlying themes and picked out the best information that would give me the big picture and get me right to the point. And I'd only have to read one book instead of 15.

That would be amazing. I would save time. And maybe my dog would be rolling over, cleaning up after my kids and doing the dishes by now. That my friend, is the reason I started smart reads. Because I wanted a company I can trust to deliver me the best information in an easy to understand way that I can digest in under an hour. Because dog training is one of many subjects I want to master.

The quicker I can learn a wide variety of topics the sooner that information can begin playing a role in shaping my future. And none of us knows how long that future will be. So why not do everything we can to make the best of it and consume a ton of knowledge. And I figured all the better if I can also make a positive difference in the world.

That's why we're also building schools, planting trees and challenging ideas about copyright's place in today's world. Because as a company we have to be doing everything we can to support the ecosystem that gives us all these beautiful places to read our books. Thanks for reading.

Travis

Customers Who Bought This

Customers Who Bought This Book Also Bought

Thrive As An Empath: How to Protect Against Psychic Vampires and Leverage Your Special Gifts

Self-Esteem Supercharger: Build Self Worth and Find Your Inner Confidence

Develop Self-Discipline: Daily Habit to Make Self Confidence and Will Power Automatic

Reinvent Yourself: Become Instantly Likable, Captivate Anyone in Seconds and Always Know What To Say

Unlimited Memory: Moonwalking with Einstein Steps to Photographic Memory

Mastering Your Time: Learn How Successful People Enhance Productivity, Beat Procrastination and Do More in Less Time

Overcoming Procrastination: Proven Strategies on How To Improve Focus, Get Things Done and Achieve Your Goals

Minimalism: Declutter, Organize and Reclaim your Space

www.ingramcontent.com/pod-product-compliance
Lightning Source LLC
Chambersburg PA
CBHW062021280526
45787CB00005B/2188